REVEALING
CHRIST

A **40-DAY** PRAYER JOURNEY FOR LENT

CHARISMA
HOUSE

Most CHARISMA HOUSE BOOK GROUP products are available at special quantity discounts for bulk purchase for sales promotions, premiums, fund-raising, and educational needs. For details, write Charisma House Book Group, 600 Rinehart Road, Lake Mary, Florida 32746, or telephone (407) 333-0600.

REVEALING CHRIST by Charisma House Editors
Published by Charisma House
Charisma Media/Charisma House Book Group
600 Rinehart Road
Lake Mary, Florida 32746
www.charismahouse.com

Unless otherwise noted, all Scripture quotations are taken from the King James Version of the Bible.

Scripture quotations marked MEV are taken from the Modern English Version. Copyright © 2014 by Military Bible Association. Used by permission. All rights reserved.

Cover design by Lisa Rae McClure
Design Director: Justin Evans

Library of Congress Control Number: 2014957970
International Standard Book Number: 978-1-62136-990-5
E-book ISBN: 978-1-62998-245-8

Portions of this book were previously published by Creation House as *The Original Maria Woodworth-Etter Devotional*, ISBN 978-0-88419-480-9, copyright © 1997; *The Original John G. Lake Devotional*, ISBN 978-0-88419-479-5, copyright © 1997; *The Original Azusa Street Devotional*, ISBN 978-0-88419-481-1, copyright © 1997; and *The*

Original Smith Wigglesworth Devotional, ISBN 978-0-88419-482-8, copyright © 1997.

First edition

15 16 17 18 19 — 987654321
Printed in the United States of America

CONTENTS

Introduction.....................................xi

Part I
The Life and Miracles of Christ

Day 1   Faith That Trusts 1

Day 2   The Baptism of a Clean Heart 4

Day 3   Radiate Christ 6

Day 4   Power in Christ 8

            Feast Sunday: *Week One of Lent*............ 11

Day 5   God's Power Shines Forth.................. 12

Day 6   In His Name 15

Day 7   Divine Healing........................... 17

Day 8   Healing and Praise 19

Day 9   Healing 21

Day 10   Believing, Pray for Healing................ 23

            Feast Sunday: *Week Two of Lent*............ 25

Day 11   Christ Formed in You...................... 26

Day 12   The Marks of the Lord Jesus................ 28

Day 13   Christ Taking Possession of Me............. 30

Day 14   Christ's Fullness in Us 32

Day 15   Abundant Life 34

Day 16   The Indwelling Christ 36

            Feast Sunday: *Week Three of Lent*........... 39

Part II
The Cross of Christ

Day 17   Crucified With Christ 43

Day 18   Overcome Pride........................... 45

Day 19   A Pure and Holy Life...................... 47

Day 20   To Die for Christ......................... 49

Day 21   Christ Our Righteousness.................. 52

Day 22   Redemption 54

         Feast Sunday: *Week Four of Lent* 57

Part III
The Resurrection and Ascension of Christ

Day 23   The Power of His Resurrection 61

Day 24   Practicing His Presence in Prayer 63

Day 25   Christ Living in You....................... 66

Day 26   Cured of Doubt and Fear................... 68

Day 27   Divine Mastery Through Christ............. 70

Day 28   Shut Out Evil............................ 72

         Feast Sunday: *Week Five of Lent* 75

Day 29   God's Resurrection Touch.................. 76

Day 30   The Vision of the Divine Reality 78

Day 31   A Life of Holy Triumph 80

Day 32   Only in Christ Is There Life 82

Day 33   Jesus's Bride 84

Day 34   Jesus Is Coming Quickly 86

Part IV
Holy Week

Palm Sunday: *Week Six of Lent*............. 91

Day 35   Not I, but Christ........................... 93

Day 36   Growing in Christ......................... 95

Day 37   Being in Prayer 97

Day 38   Even Unto Death.......................... 99

Day 39   Victory Follows Crucifixion 101

Day 40   Praying the Cross 103

Resurrection Day......................... 105

INTRODUCTION

THE LIFE, DEATH, and resurrection of the Lord Jesus Christ are the three most earth-shattering events in all of human history. Christians, regardless of denomination, culture, or geographic location, are brought into unity under these three events. It is our faith in these events and what they do in our lives that make us one, that make us followers of Christ. As the Holy Spirit gives us fuller revelation of the impact of Christ on humanity, we experience His beauty and His glory, changing us forever.

We invite you to take an intentional and intimate journey to come in contact once again with the miraculous, beautiful, and sacrificial life of Christ. We chose to center this experience around the forty-day season before Easter or Resurrection Day, because it is a time Christians all over the world begin to focus on the impact Christ made on our eternity. This time is traditionally called Lent. However, we have provided only a framework, a template, if you will. Our prayer is that you will partner with the Spirit of God to discover how to use this resource in the way that best allows you to encounter a new understanding of who Jesus is to you.

Accompanying you on this journey are the actual words and teachings of great men and women of God such as:

- Maria Woodworth-Etter, who ministered with the power of the Holy Spirit in the nineteenth century. She was one of the first Pentecostal women in America to preach and teach the gospel.

- William J. Seymour, who was the son of ex-slaves but a passionate believer of racial integration. Blind in one eye yet in possession of remarkable vision, Seymour led the Azusa Street Revival in Los Angeles in 1906 and is credited for launching the twentieth-century American Pentecostal movement and several denominations.

- John G. Lake, whose ministry was marked by extraordinary miracles. His writings were anointed and faith-filled.

- Smith Wigglesworth, a powerful prayer warrior whose ministry touched thousands of people in the early part of the twentieth century. Wherever he ministered, miracles, signs, and wonders would follow.

Combined with a daily Scripture verse, points to ponder, and a short prayer, these timeless and Spirit-filled revelations into the life of Christ will activate the full expression of the gospel in your life and revive a hunger for God's Spirit to empower you to do great things.

So whether you observe Lent or in your own way commemorate the days leading up to the Cross and Resurrection, and whether the Spirit leads you to fast or feast, we pray that at the end of the forty days you are drawn into a deep place of intimacy, devotion, and authentic faith.

May your time with God be enhanced during this season. May you forever be changed in the light of His glorious Son, never to be the same again.

—CHARISMA HOUSE EDITORS

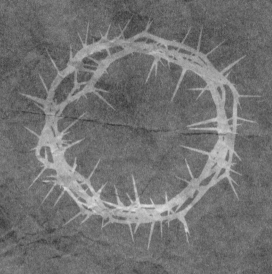

PART I

THE LIFE AND
MIRACLES OF CHRIST

Day 1

FAITH THAT TRUSTS

We have such trust through Christ toward God, not that we are sufficient in ourselves to take credit for anything ourselves, but our sufficiency is from God.

[2 CORINTHIANS 3:4–5, MEV]

WE WANT TO get to a place where we are beyond trusting ourselves. Beloved, there is so much failure in self-assurances. It is not bad to have good things on the lines of satisfaction, but we must never have anything on the human plane that we rest upon.

There is only one sure place to rest upon, and our trust is in God. In Thy name we go. In Thee we trust. And God brings us off in victory. When we have no confidence in ourselves to trust in our God, He has promised to be with us at all times, to make the path straight, and to make a way. Then we understand how it is that David could say, "Thy gentleness hath made me great" (2 Sam. 22:36).

Ah, thou Lover of souls! We have no confidence in the flesh. Our confidence can only stand and rely on the One who is able to come in at the midnight hour as easily as at noonday and make the night and the day alike to the man who rests completely in the will of God, knowing that "all things work together for good to them that love God" and trust Him. And such trust have we in Him. The Lord has helped me to have no confidence in myself but to trust wholly in Him. Bless His name!

—SMITH WIGGLESWORTH

POINTS TO PONDER

True faith moves us from trusting in a life preserver to trusting in a lifesaver. What does this mean? A life preserver is something that we hold on to with all our strength. But if no lifesaver comes to our rescue, our strength will eventually fail and we will be lost. A lifesaver is a person who comes to rescue us. They take us from danger to safety, from deep water to dry ground, from near death to life.

Everything in life is merely a life preserver. On this Ash Wednesday it is important for us to remember that everything is as dust—from dust we were created and to dust we shall return. Only Jesus is a lifesaver. Only Jesus has the power to save.

- When it comes to saving tactics, what do you often hold on to in order to survive or save yourself (i.e., money, people, career, etc.)?

- Our confidence and trust is totally in Jesus Christ. Read the following verses and write in a journal how your trust in Christ is grounded in total confidence:

  - Psalm 27:1–3
  - Psalm 118:8–9
  - Proverbs 3:26
  - Proverbs 14:26
  - 2 Corinthians 5:6–8
  - Ephesians 3:11–12
  - Philippians 1:6
  - Hebrews 3:6, 14

- • 1 John 3:21
- • 1 John 5:14

• Are you trusting in a life preserver or in the true lifesaver? Is your confidence in your own ability or in the Lord?

PRAY...

Lord, in You alone I place my trust and my confidence. Amen.

Day 2
THE BAPTISM OF A CLEAN HEART

Jesus, being filled with the Holy Spirit,
returned from the Jordan and was led
by the Spirit into the wilderness.

[LUKE 4:1, MEV]

JESUS IS OUR example. Upon His clean heart, the baptism fell. We find in reading the Bible that the baptism with the Holy Ghost and fire falls on a clean, sanctified life. For we see, according to the Scriptures, that Jesus was filled with wisdom and favor with God and man before God anointed Him with the Holy Ghost and power. For in Luke 2:40, we read, "[Jesus] waxed strong in spirit, filled with wisdom: and the grace of God was upon him." Then in Luke 2:52, "And Jesus increased in wisdom and stature, and in favour with God and man."

After Jesus was empowered with the Holy Ghost at Jordan, He returned in the power of the Spirit into Galilee, and there went out a fame of Him through all the region round about. He was not any more holy or any more meek but had greater authority: "And he taught in their synagogues, being glorified of all" (Luke 4:15).

Beloved, if Jesus, who was God Himself, needed the Holy Ghost to empower Him for His ministry and His miracles, how much more do we children need the Holy Ghost baptism today. Oh, that men and women would tarry for the baptism with the Holy Ghost and fire upon their souls!

—WILLIAM J. SEYMOUR

POINTS TO PONDER

Jesus was empowered by the Holy Spirit for ministry. Below is a list of the ways Luke's Gospel says He was empowered by the Spirit.

Jesus was…

- Conceived by the Spirit (Luke 1:35)
- Descended upon by the Spirit (Luke 3:22)
- Filled with the Spirit (Luke 4:1)
- Led by the Spirit (Luke 4:1)
- Empowered by the Spirit (Luke 4:14)
- Anointed by the Spirit (Luke 4:18)
- Filled with the Spirit's joy (Luke 10:21)

- What Spirit empowerments have you experienced in your own Christian walk? How have you seen the Spirit at work in your life previously?

- Are you doing anything in your life to hinder the Spirit right now?

- How do you desire the Spirit to touch your life right now?

PRAY…

God, cleanse my heart with Your fire, that I may receive the baptism of Your Spirit. Amen.

Day 3
RADIATE CHRIST

For this purpose the Son of God was revealed,
that He might destroy the works of the devil.
[1 JOHN 3:8, MEV]

EVIL IS REAL. The devil is real. He was a real angel. Pride changed his nature.

God is real. The operation of God within the heart changes our nature until we are new creations in Christ Jesus, new creatures in Christ Jesus. The power of God, the Holy Ghost, is the Spirit of dominion. It makes the believer a child of God. It makes one not subject to the forces of the world or the flesh or the devil. These are under the Christian's feet.

Beloved, God wants us to come, to stay, and to live in that abiding place, which is the Christian's estate. This is the heavenly place in Christ Jesus. This is the secret place of the Most High. Bless God!

The Word of God gives us this key. It says, "That wicked one toucheth him not" (1 John 5:18). When the Spirit of God radiated from the man Jesus, I wonder how close to Him it was possible for the evil spirit to come? Do you not see that the Spirit of God is as destructive of evil as it is creative of good? It was impossible for the evil one to come near Him, and I feel sure Satan talked to Jesus from a safe distance.

The Spirit of God radiates from the Christian's person because of the indwelling Holy Ghost and makes him impregnable to any touch or contact of evil forces. He is the subjective force himself. The Spirit of God radiates from him as long as his faith in God is active. "Resist the devil, and he will flee from you" (James 4:7).

—JOHN G. LAKE

POINTS TO PONDER

- When Christ was tempted in the desert (Matt. 4:1–11), He demonstrated an ability to withstand temptation and overcome the evil one. What is it like for you to be tempted by the evil one? How do you usually respond?

- What kind of help do you need when you are being tempted?

- If you were to write out a prayer for help, asking God for those things you need in your moments of temptation, what would it say? Write it in your prayer journal.

PRAY...

Jesus, radiate through me with Your power to destroy the works of the devil around about me. Amen.

Day 4
POWER IN CHRIST

He who is in you is greater than
he who is in the world.

[1 JOHN 4:4, MEV]

A PERSON WITH CHRIST within by the Holy Ghost is greater than any other power in the world. All other natural and evil powers are less than God. Satan is a lesser power.

Man with God in him is greater than Satan. That is the reason that God tells the believer that he shall be able to cast out devils. The Christian, therefore, is a ruler. He is in the place of dominion, the place of authority, even as Jesus was. Jesus, knowing that all power had been given unto Him, took a basin and a towel and washed His disciples' feet. His power did not exalt Him. It made Him the humblest of all men.

So the more a Christian possesses Christ's power, the more of a servant he will be. God is the great servant of the world. He is the One who continually gives to men the necessity of the hour. Through His guidance and direction of the laws of the world, He provides for all the needs of mankind. He is the great servant of the world, the greatest of all servants.

Yes, Jesus, knowing that all power had been committed to Him, commits through the Holy Ghost, by His own Spirit, all power to man.

—JOHN G. LAKE

Points to Ponder

- What is it like for you to consider having a greater power within yourself, through the Holy Spirit's presence in you, than any other power in the world?

- How do you access the power of the Holy Spirit in your life?

- In what ways do you demonstrate the servantlike authority of Christ? How is your power turned into humility?

Pray...

Lord Jesus, grant me the strength and courage to walk in the power You have given me. Amen.

FEAST SUNDAY

Week One of Lent

IN THESE FIRST few days of Lent we have stepped over the threshold of Ash Wednesday, which reminded us of our mortality and the fleeting nature of all that exists in this life, and we have considered the power Christ took with Him into the desert and exercised during His own forty-day fast in the wilderness. On this first Feast Sunday of the Lenten period, when we take a break from fasting, take some time for reflection on the days you've completed.

- What have the first few days of this forty-day period of Lent been like for you?

- What have you noticed or learned about Christ so far in this study?

- What have you learned about yourself?

- What have you learned about the enemy of your soul?

- What is your hope for the remainder of this Lenten season?

Day 5
GOD'S POWER SHINES FORTH

Go and tell John what you hear and see.

[MATTHEW 11:4, MEV]

WHAT A WONDERFUL people we are in our privileges! Today everyone may be God's priest. If we abide in Him and His words abide in us, we may ask what we will and it shall be done. We indeed have wonderful privileges. The power of the Lord shines forth a hundred times greater than under the law.

When John was in prison, he began to doubt whether Jesus was the Christ, and he sent his disciples to ask, "Art Thou He that should come?" Jesus did not say, "I belong to the church or I belong to a college." He told John's disciples to tell John the things they had seen—the lame walked, the blind could see, different diseases were healed, and the poor had the gospel preached to them.

If John did not believe in Christ through the signs, no eloquence would be of value. If he did not believe what the witnesses told him, he would not believe anything.

Neither will you! If you only look on, it will seem foolishness to you as we praise God, get filled with the Holy Ghost, and get gifts. But it is Jesus first, last, and all the time. We hold up Jesus and praise His name. We see bright, happy faces. We see pain go out of bodies, and we go home rejoicing.

—MARIA WOODWORTH-ETTER

POINTS TO PONDER

Miracles are signs that point to God's acting in history. If a miracle points to a man or institution, then it is counterfeit. When unbelievers encounter God's miracles, they are either awed by His power or angry. Why? Because men are always humbled when God acts. So prideful human intellect always hates God's miracles.

We often hear the well-known phrase asserted, "Expect a miracle!" Jesus seems to have put a slightly differently slant on this perspective: "Expect Jesus!" When you expect Jesus, then miracles happen. So go beyond expecting miracles to expecting the God of all miracles to act in love and grace.

- Read Mark 7:1–23 and then summarize in your prayer journal the description Jesus gave of the kind of heart that is against God's ways.

- When you witness a miracle from God, how do you respond? List all your responses or feelings in your prayer journal.

  - Joy
  - Pride
  - Anger
  - Doubt
  - Hope
  - Praise
  - Frustration
  - Jealousy
  - Awe

- Wonder
- Amazement
- Fear

- How are your eyes and ears open to the miracles of God?

PRAY...

Lord Jesus, help me to move beyond the traditions of men and into Your power, signs, and wonders. Amen.

Day 6
IN HIS NAME

Whatever you ask the Father in My
name, He will give it to you.
[JOHN 16:23, MEV]

MATCHLESS NAME! THE secret of power was in it. When the disciples used the name, the power struck. The dynamite of heaven exploded. Peter and John were hustled off to jail. The church prayed for them "in the name." They were released. They went to the church.

The entire church prayed that signs and wonders might be done. How did they pray? "In the name." They used it legally. The vital response was instantaneous. The place was shaken as by an earthquake. Tremendous name!

Jesus commanded: "Go into all the world." Why? To proclaim the name. To use the name. In it was concentrated the combined authority resident in the Father, the Son, and the Holy Ghost.

The apostles used the name. It worked. The deacons at Samaria used the name. The fire flashed. Believers everywhere, forever, were commanded to use it. The name detonated around the world.

Prayer in His name gets answers. The Moravians prayed. The greatest revival till that time hit the world. Finney prayed. America rocked with power. Hudson Taylor prayed. China's Inland Mission was born. Evan Roberts prayed seven years. The Welsh revival resulted.

Pray in the name of Jesus!

—JOHN G. LAKE

POINTS TO PONDER

When we pray in the name of Jesus, we are praying in His will, power, and authority. Nothing happens when we pray in any other name but His!

- Read these scriptures and write down in your prayer journal what they reveal about the power of the name of Jesus:

  - Matthew 18:20
  - Mark 9:39
  - Luke 9:48
  - John 14:13
  - John 16:23–26
  - Acts 3:16
  - Acts 4:12
  - Colossians 3:17

- Make a list of all the people and things you need to pray about in His name.

- What hinders you from praying in Christ's name?

PRAY...

In Your name, Lord Jesus, I pray for the fire of Your Holy Spirit to baptize me. Amen.

Day 7
DIVINE HEALING

For I am the LORD who heals you.

[EXODUS 15:26, MEV]

IN DIVINE HEALING today, the unchangeableness of God's eternal purpose is thereby demonstrated. "Jesus Christ the same yesterday, and to day, and for ever" (Heb. 13:8). "I am the LORD, I change not" (Mal. 3:6).

God always was the healer. He is the healer still, and will ever remain the healer. Healing is for you. Jesus healed all that came to Him. He never turned anyone away. He never said, "It is not God's will to heal you," or that it was better for the individual to remain sick, or that they were being perfected in character through the sickness. Jesus healed them all, thereby demonstrating forever God's unchangeable will concerning sickness and healing.

Have you need of healing? Pray to God in the name of Jesus Christ to remove the disease. Command it to leave you as you would sin. Assert your divine authority and refuse to have it. Jesus purchased your freedom from sickness as He purchased your freedom from sin.

—JOHN G. LAKE

POINTS TO PONDER

- Supernatural healing is regarded as a mixed bag these days. Some believe it can happen. Some have experienced it firsthand. Still others are skeptical. What do you believe about healing?

- If you could ask Christ to heal anything or anyone right now, what or who would it be?

- What questions do you have about the healing power of Christ?

PRAY...

Jesus, by Your power and authority, I am healed. Amen.

Day 8
HEALING AND PRAISE

Immediately he rose, picked up the bed,
and went out in front of them all, so that
they were all amazed and glorified God,
saying, "We never saw anything like this!"

[MARK 2:12, MEV]

THE PARALYTIC DID not break up the meeting when he was brought to Jesus and dropped down through the roof while Jesus was preaching. Jesus is our example. He was glad to have something like that happen, because it gave Him a chance to show His power. Jesus forgave the man all his sins and then made him rise, take up his bed, and walk.

The people began to shout, "Glory," the same way you do here. You cannot help it. If you have not done it, you will. A consumptive woman was brought [into a meeting] in her night robe. I did not care what she had on—she was healed. Hallelujah!

When the paralytic was healed, they gave glory to God. People say today, "You never heard such a noisy group." If they had only heard them then! We have something to make a fuss about. Dead people never make much noise, do they? There is not much noise in a graveyard!

—MARIA WOODWORTH-ETTER

POINTS TO PONDER

Expect more than a miracle. Expect Jesus to pour out and baptize you with His Holy Spirit. When you have His presence in your life, your life is lived within the miracle-potent atmosphere of the Holy Spirit.

- How would you define a miracle?

- What miracles have you witnessed?

- What miracle do you want to see in your life now?

- Write out a prayer asking Christ to demonstrate His miracle-working power in that area of your life.

PRAY...

Jesus, I praise You for Your healing and delivering. Amen.

Day 9
HEALING

Is anyone sick among you? Let him call for the
elders of the church, and let them pray over him,
anointing him with oil in the name of the Lord.

[JAMES 5:14, MEV]

JESUS STILL HEALS today. Praise God! Jesus said, "Men ought always to pray, and not to faint" (Luke 18:1). Many precious children of God today, instead of praying, commence grieving. But God's Word says, "Let him pray." And if we obey His Word, He will heal us. We read in Psalm 107:20, "He sent his word, and healed them, and delivered them from their destructions." And we read in Proverbs 4:20, "My son, attend to my words; incline thine ear unto my sayings."

Jesus is speaking through the power of the Holy Ghost to every believer to keep His precious Word. "Let them not depart from thine eyes; keep them in the midst of thine heart. For they are life unto those that find them, and health to all their flesh" (Prov. 4:21–22).

We read in Exodus 15:26, "I am the LORD that healeth thee." Jesus said, "And as Moses lifted up the serpent in the wilderness, even so must the Son of man be lifted up: that whosoever believeth in him should not perish, but have eternal life" (John 3:14–15).

Dear beloved, we see in receiving the words of Jesus, it brings not only life to our souls and spirits but to these physical bodies. For His words are medicine to our bodies through faith.

—WILLIAM J. SEYMOUR

POINTS TO PONDER

One manifestation of the Spirit's moving in revival is healing. God heals, delivers, saves, and sets us free when He moves in power. Write down what the Word reveals about His healing:

- Exodus 15:26
- Psalm 103:3
- Psalm 107:20
- Jeremiah 17:14
- Mark 6:13
- James 5:14–15

- God revives us physically, emotionally, mentally, and spiritually with His healing power. Do you need His healing? Complete the following sentences and write them in your prayer journal.

  - I need His physical healing for...
  - I need His emotional healing for...
  - I need His intellectual healing for...
  - I need His spiritual healing for...

PRAY...

Jesus, You are the Great Physician. Anoint me with the oil of Your healing. Amen.

Day 10
BELIEVING, PRAY FOR HEALING

Whatever things you ask when you pray, believe
that you will receive them, and you will have them.
[MARK 11:24, MEV]

THERE IS NO question in the mind of God concerning the salvation of a sinner. No more is there question concerning the healing of the sick one. It is in the atonement of Jesus Christ, bless God. His atonement was unto the uttermost, to the last need of man.

The responsibility rests purely, solely, and entirely on man. Jesus put it there. Jesus said, "When ye pray, believe that ye receive them, and ye shall have them." No questions or ifs in the words of Jesus. If He ever spoke with emphasis on any question, it was on the subject of God's will and the result of faith in prayer. Indeed, He did not even speak them in ordinary words but in the custom of the East. He said, "Verily, verily." Amen, amen—the same as if I were to stand in an American court and say, "I swear to tell the truth, the whole truth, and nothing but the truth, so help me God."

So instead of praying, "Lord, if it be Thy will," when you kneel beside your sick friend, Jesus Christ has commanded you and every believer to lay your hands on the sick. This is not my ministry nor my brethren's only. It is the ministry of every believer. And if your ministers do not believe it, God have mercy on them. If your churches do not believe it, God have mercy on them.

—JOHN G. LAKE

POINTS TO PONDER

Remember, God's healing does not rest in the power of your faith but in the power of His faithfulness. He does not ask you to trust your praying but to trust Him, who answers your prayers.

The responsibility to pray for the healing of others rests entirely on us. Consider this: What if God's healing is not released in another's life because we did not pray? How many could be healed if you prayed? How many are not being healed because of your prayerlessness?

- What keeps you from trusting Him for healing?

  - Past experience
  - Pain
  - Hurt
  - Fear
  - Unbelief
  - Ignorance of the Word
  - Other

- In your prayer journal make a list of all those whom you know who need healing—physical, emotional, or relational—and the kind of healing they need.

- How willing are you to pray for those who need healing?

PRAY...

Lord, give me the boldness to pray for all the sick that I meet, believing Your will for their healing. Amen.

FEAST SUNDAY

Week Two of Lent

I N THIS PAST week of our Lenten journey, we've explored the healing power and miraculous work of Christ. What's more, we've considered that this healing and miracle-working power is yet available to us today. On this Feast Sunday, take some time to reflect on the journey through the healing aspect of Christ you explored this past week.

- What roles have healing and miracles played in your faith journey?

- What has it been like for you to consider the healing power of Christ available to you today?

- What would it be like for Christ to effect healing for others through you?

- What final thoughts on healing and miracles would you like to voice right now?

Express your thoughts in your prayer journal.

Day 11
CHRIST FORMED IN YOU

...until we all come into the unity of
the faith and...to the measure of the
stature of the fullness of Christ.
[EPHESIANS 4:13, MEV]

THIS SCRIPTURE SHOWS the ultimate purpose of Christ as Savior, of Christ as a companion, of Christ as the indwelling One. Christ's presence with us is not just as an outward companion but an indwelling, divine force revolutionizing our nature and making us like Him. Indeed, the final and ultimate purpose of the Christ is that the Christian shall be reproduced in His own likeness, within and without.

Paul expressed the same thing in the first chapter of Colossians, where he says, "To present you holy and unblameable and unreprovable in his sight" (v. 22). That transformation is to be an inner transformation. It is a transformation of our life, of our nature into His nature, into His likeness.

How wonderful the patience, how marvelous the power that takes possession of the soul of man and accomplishes the will of God—an absolute transformation into the beautiful holiness of the character of Jesus. Our heart staggers when we think of such a calling, when we think of such a nature, when we contemplate such a character. That is God's purpose for you and me.

In emphasizing this truth, the apostle again puts it into a different form. He says, "Until Christ be formed in you" (Gal. 4:19).

That is the mission of the Lord Jesus Christ. That is the

marvel He works in our lives—to transform the soul into the likeness and character of Himself and then present us to the Father, "holy and unblameable and unreprovable in his sight" (Col. 1:22).

—JOHN G. LAKE

POINTS TO PONDER

When you think about the ultimate purpose of Christ, what do you imagine? Saving us from sin and death, perhaps? Teaching us about life everlasting and the kingdom? Yes, those things are true. But even more, Christ wants to change your nature. You are meant to become a new creation, ever more and more like Him.

- What comes to mind when you think of Christ's nature?

- What will it would look like for your nature to become more and more like Christ's? How would the person you are today be changed?

- On a scale of one to five, with five being very open, how open are you to having your nature changed? Why is that?

PRAY...

Lord Jesus, by Your grace, transform me into Your likeness. Amen.

Day 12
THE MARKS OF THE LORD JESUS

I bear in my body the marks of the Lord Jesus.
[GALATIANS 6:17, MEV]

Y OU NOTICE AMONG the most devout Christians how continuously their thought is limited to that place where they can be exercised or moved by God. But God's best is more than that.

While I was in Chicago, I met a couple of old friends who invited me to dinner. While at dinner, the lady, who is a very frank woman, said: "Mr. Lake, I have known you so long and have had such close fellowship with you for so many years that I am able to speak very frankly."

I said, "Yes, absolutely."

"Well," she said, "there is something I miss about you. For lack of words, I am going to put it in Paul's words: 'I bear in my body the marks of the Lord Jesus' (Gal. 6:17). You do not seem to have the marks of Jesus."

I said, "That depends whether or not it is the marks of mannerisms. If you are expecting that the personality that God gave me is going to be changed so that I am going to be another fellow and not myself, then you will miss it. If that is the kind of marks you are looking for, you will not find them.

"But if you are expecting to observe a man's flesh and blood and bones and spirit and mind indwelt by God, then you will find them—not a machine, not an automaton or an imitation, but a clear mind and a pure heart, a son of God in nature and essence."

All God's effort with the world is to bring out the real man in the image of Christ, that real man with the knowledge of God. That real man, reconstructed until his very substance is the substance of God.

—John G. Lake Points to Ponder

It's an interesting way to think about it, isn't it—that becoming more like Christ doesn't mean becoming a completely different person entirely? We will still be ourselves, just more godlike, more filled with Christ's way of being.

- How do you respond to the idea that you're not meant to become someone different from yourself as you are fashioned more and more into Christ's image?

- What do you think it will look like for you to grow into being the same person you are but one who has the same substance of God?

- How would you describe the substance of God?

- How is God's substance different from your substance today?

Pray...

I desire to bear Your marks, Lord Jesus, in my body. Manifest Your vision and touch in me. Amen.

Day 13

CHRIST TAKING POSSESSION OF ME

I will greatly rejoice in the LORD, my soul shall be joyful in my God; for He has clothed me with the garments of salvation.

[ISAIAH 61:10, MEV]

THE SPIRIT OF God is a force that takes possession of the nature of man and works in man the will of God. The will of God is ever to make man like Himself. Blessed be His precious name.

It would be a strange Word, indeed, and a strange salvation if Jesus was not able to produce from the whole race one man in His own image, in His own likeness, and of His own character. We would think that salvation was weak, would we not?

If the world were nothing but cripples, as it largely is, soul cripples, physical cripples, mental cripples everywhere, then I want to know what kind of a conception the world has received of the divinity of Jesus Christ, of the power of His salvation? Is there no hope, is there no way out of the difficulty, is there no force that can lift the soul of man into union with God so that once again the life of God thrills in his members?

The mere fact of a brother's deliverance from suffering and inability to help himself and a possible premature death is a very small matter in itself in comparison with the wonder it reveals to us. The revelation of the power of God at the command of man to be applied to the destruction of evil, whether spiritual or physical, mental or psychological, shows us Christ's purpose and desire to bring man by the grace of God once more into his heavenly estate, where he recognizes himself a son of God. Blessed be His Name.

—JOHN G. LAKE

POINTS TO PONDER

When we think about the power of Christ's salvation, we often think of the power it brings to save our souls from death. This is truly part of Christ's power to save us. But we are also presented here with the idea that Christ's salvation is about making us more and more into His own image.

- How is being made into the image of Christ a form of salvation?

- In what ways have you experienced the Spirit of God taking possession of you?

- How have you seen your nature change over the course of your life in God?

PRAY...

How I rejoice, O Lord, that You are transforming me into Your image. Amen.

Day 14
CHRIST'S FULLNESS IN US

*...until we all come into the unity of the
faith and of the knowledge of the Son
of God, into a complete man, to the measure of the stature of the fullness of Christ.*

[EPHESIANS 4:13, MEV]

EXPERIMENTALLY, I KNEW God as Savior from sin. I knew
the power of the Christ within my own heart to keep me
above the power of temptation and to help me live a godly life.
But when the purpose of God in the salvation of man first
dawned upon my soul, that is, when the greatness of it dawned
upon my soul, life became for me a grand, new thing.

By the study of God's Word and by the revelation of His
Spirit, it became a fact in my soul that God's purpose was no
less in me than it was in the Lord Jesus. His purpose is no less
in you and I, as younger brethren, than it was in Jesus Christ,
our elder brother. Then I saw the purpose that God had in
mind for the human race. Then I saw the greatness of Jesus's
desire, that desire that was so intense it caused Him, as King
of Glory, to lay down all that glory possessed for Him and
come to earth to be born as a man. He joined hands with our
humanity and, by His grace, lifts us in consciousness and life
to the same level that He Himself enjoyed.

Christ became a new factor in my soul. A vision of His
purpose thrilled my being. I could understand then how Jesus
approached man and his needs at the very bottom, calling
mankind to Him. Then, by His loving touch and the power of

the Spirit through His Word, He destroyed the sickness and sin that bound man and set us free both in body and in soul.

—JOHN G. LAKE

POINTS TO PONDER

- What is it like for you to consider God's purpose in you being no less than it was in Christ?

- What might that purpose be?

PRAY...

My prayer, Lord Jesus, is all of You in all of me, Your fullness in me. Amen.

Day 15
ABUNDANT LIFE

The thief does not come, except to steal and kill and destroy. I came that they may have life, and that they may have it more abundantly.

[JOHN 10:10, MEV]

THERE IS A quickening by the Spirit of God so that one's body, soul, or mind and spirit all alike may become blessed, pervaded, and filled with the presence of God Himself. The Word of God is wonderfully clear along these lines. For instance, the Word of God asserts, "Thou wilt keep him in perfect peace, whose mind is stayed on thee" (Isa. 26:3). Why? "Because he trusteth in thee." That is the rest that a Christian knows whose mind has perfect trust in God.

The Word of God says that our hearts will rejoice and our flesh will rest in hope (Ps. 16:9). Not our mind, but our very flesh shall hope and rest in God. God is to be a living presence not only in the spirit of man nor in the mind of man alone, but also in the flesh of man so that God is known in all departments of life. We know God in our very flesh. We know God in our mind. We know God in our spirit.

The medium by which God undertakes to bless the world is through the transmission of Himself. The Spirit of God is His own substance, the substance of His being, the very nature and quality of the presence, being, and nature of God.

That is the secret of the abundant life of which Jesus spoke. The reason we have the more abundant life is because that by receiving God into our being, all the springs of our being are quickened by His living presence.

—John G. Lake

Points to Ponder

The life we know with God is meant to be holistic. It's meant to invade every aspect of our lives—not just our outer world, but our inner world as well. You are meant to be changed in every respect of your being.

- How have you experienced transformation in your mind by the presence of God?

- How have you experienced transformation in your heart by the presence of God?

- How have you experienced transformation in your spirit by the presence of God?

- How have you experienced transformation in your flesh by the presence of God?

Pray...

Fill me, Spirit of God, with Your life, that I might rest in Your hope and rejoice in You. Amen.

Day 16
THE INDWELLING CHRIST

He called His twelve disciples to Him
and gave them authority…
[MATTHEW 10:1, MEV]

BELOVED, HE GIVES it to you. What is the Holy Ghost? It is the gift of God Himself to you. The Holy Spirit is not simply given that you may be a channel and always a channel. No, sir! The most magnificent thing the Word of God portrays is that Christ, indwelling in you by the Holy Ghost, makes you a son of God like Jesus Christ, with the recognized power of God in your spirit to command the will of God.

It may not be that all souls have grown to that place where such a life as that is evident, but surely if the Son of God by the Holy Ghost has been born in our heart, it is time we began to let Him have some degree of sway in our heart and some degree of heavenly dominion of value and some degree of the lightnings of Jesus Christ breaking forth from our spirit.

The sanest man is the man who believes God and stands on His promises, knows the secret of His power, receives the Holy Ghost, gives Him sway in his life, and goes out in the name of the Lord Jesus to command the will of God and bring it to pass in the world.

—JOHN G. LAKE

POINTS TO PONDER

It is not just the life of Christ we are meant to examine and come to emulate. It is also the Holy Spirit. This is the power that lives inside us and changes us from the inside. This is the power that makes our nature into the nature of Christ. This is the reality of God come near—even nearer than Christ when He came to earth.

- How do you experience the reality of the Holy Spirit in your life?

- What power has been given to you through the Spirit's presence?

PRAY...

Spirit of God, use me to set others free from the powers of sickness and unclean spirits through the name of Jesus. Amen.

FEAST SUNDAY
Week Three of Lent

I N THIS PAST week of our Lenten study, we've been exploring the reality of Christ's nature coming to live in us. Take some time to reflect on how this concept has become real to you this week.

- Prior to this week's study how much did this concept of Christ's nature becoming your nature reflect your understanding of God's purpose for you?

- How would you describe the way this change in your nature occurs?

- What do you most desire when it comes to taking on the nature of Christ?

- Write a prayer in your journal that shares with God your desire for this reality to become more real in your life.

PART II

THE CROSS OF CHRIST

Day 17
CRUCIFIED WITH CHRIST

I have been crucified with Christ. It is no longer I who live, but Christ who lives in me. And the life I now live in the flesh, I live by faith in the Son of God.

[GALATIANS 2:20, MEV]

JESUS IS SEARCHING for a people who will believe the gospel. He has never changed the gospel in any way since He commissioned it. Many take sanctification to be the power. They stop when they have the original sin taken out and Christ has been enthroned on their hearts. But God wants us to go on to be filled with the Holy Ghost, that we may be witnesses unto Him to the uttermost parts of the earth.

The times of ignorance God winked at, but now He commands men everywhere to repent. The Lord is restoring all the gifts to His church. He wants people everywhere to repent. He wants a people who have faith in His Word and in the Holy Spirit.

Jesus was not only nailed to the cross but hung there until He died. He did not come down from the cross as they told Him to do, though He had the power to do so. So with us. When we are crucified with Christ, we should not come down and live for self again but stay on the cross. A constant death to self is the way to follow our Master.

—WILLIAM J. SEYMOUR

POINTS TO PONDER

Christ is our best example of what it means to die to self. Besides the literal death He underwent on the cross, we also see the way His life was filled with opportunities to practice this way of life. He demonstrated dying to self when choosing to wash His disciples' feet. He died to His own preferences and comforts by traveling from city to city and serving multitudes of people in need. We see Him give up His wish to avoid the cross while praying in the Garden of Gethsemane. And He invites us to live this same way in the world.

- Would you describe yourself as having died to self? If not, why not?

- What keeps you from dying to self?

  - Fear of losing control
  - Unbelief
  - Desire to continue in past sin
  - Unconfessed sin
  - Ignorance
  - Anything else?

- What do you think it will take for you to surrender all?

PRAY...

Lord, I desire to be crucified to self so that I may live totally for You. Amen.

Day 18
OVERCOME PRIDE

Let this mind be in you all, which was
also in Christ Jesus, who, being in
the form of God…humbled Himself
and became obedient to death.
[PHILIPPIANS 2:5–6, 8, MEV]

AT HIS LAST Supper with the disciples, knowing that all power had been given unto Him, Jesus took a towel and a basin and proceeded to wash the disciples' feet. When He had finished, He said, "Know ye what I have done to you?" (John 13:12). In explanation, He said, "If I then, your Lord and Master, have washed your feet; ye also ought to wash one another's feet" (v. 14).

When we examine the human heart and endeavor to discover what it is that retards our progress, I believe we will find that pride in the human soul is perhaps the greatest difficulty we have to overcome. Jesus taught us a wonderful humility, taking the place of a servant. We are enjoined to thus treat and love one another.

His presence with us, His presence in us must produce in our hearts the same conditions that were in His own. It must bring into our life the same humility that was in Him. It is one of the secrets of entrance into the grace of God.

—JOHN G. LAKE

POINTS TO PONDER

Pride can be the greatest deterrent to our growing close to God. It is what led to Satan's downfall from heaven, where he was as close to God as any living being could imagine. It keeps us at a distance, creating walls in the heart, and we don't ultimately receive what we're looking for.

- Where do you see evidence of pride in your life?

- Why do you think that pride is there?

- How do you respond to the invitation to let your pride go and embrace humility instead?

- If you were to write out a prayer to God concerning pride and humility, what would it say?

PRAY...

Lord Jesus, teach me to be a servant even as You served. Amen.

Matt 6:1-8

Day 19
A PURE AND HOLY LIFE

For both He who sanctifies and those who
are sanctified are all of One. For this reason
He is not ashamed to call them brothers.
[HEBREWS 2:11, MEV]

IN ORDER TO live a pure and holy life, one does not need the baptism of the Holy Ghost. The Holy Ghost does not cleanse anyone from sin. It is Jesus's shed blood on Calvary that cleanses us from sin. The Holy Ghost never died for our sins. It was Jesus who died for our sins, and it is His blood that atones.

"If we walk in the light, as he is in the light, we have fellowship one with another, and the blood of Jesus Christ his Son cleanseth us from all sin…If we confess our sins, he is faithful and just to forgive us our sins, and to cleanse us from all unrighteousness" (1 John 1:7, 9). It is the blood that cleanses and makes holy, and through the blood we receive the baptism of the Holy Spirit. The Holy Ghost always falls in response to the blood.

—WILLIAM J. SEYMOUR

POINTS TO PONDER

The blood of Jesus Christ cleanses and purifies us while opening the door to the Spirit of God and revival. The effective power of His blood paves the way for personal forgiveness and renewal.

- What role does the blood of Christ play in your understanding of your faith?

- How would you describe the relationship between Christ's blood and the Holy Spirit?

- Read the following passages and jot down in your prayer journal what each says about the power of the blood to affect your life:

  - John 6:55–56
  - Romans 3:25
  - Romans 5:9
  - Ephesians 1:7
  - Ephesians 2:13
  - Colossians 1:14–20
  - Hebrews 9:20–25
  - Hebrews 13:12–20
  - 1 Peter 1:17–20
  - 1 John 1:7–9

PRAY...

Jesus, cleanse and purify me with Your blood. Amen.

Day 20
TO DIE FOR CHRIST

For to me, to continue living is
Christ, and to die is gain.
[PHILIPPIANS 1:21, MEV]

DEAR FRIENDS, THERE is not an authentic history that can tell us whether any one of the disciples died a natural death. We know that at least nine of them were martyrs, possibly all. Peter died on a cross; James was beheaded; the Romans did not even wait to make a cross for Thomas—they nailed him to an olive tree. John was sentenced to be executed at Ephesus by being placed in a caldron of boiling oil. God delivered him, his executioners refused to repeat the operation, and he was banished to the Isle of Patmos.

John thought so little about it that he never tells of the incident. He says only, "I…was in the isle that is called Patmos, for the word of God, and for the testimony of Jesus Christ" (Rev. 1:9).

Friends, the group of missionaries that followed me went without food and clothes, and once when one of my preachers was sunstruck and had wandered away, I tracked him by the blood marks of his feet. That is the kind of consecration that established Pentecost in South Africa.

If I were pledging men and women to the gospel of the Son of God, as I am endeavoring to do now, it would not be to have a nice church and harmonious surroundings and a sweet do-nothing time. I would invite them to be ready to die. That was the spirit of early Methodism. John Wesley established a heroic call. He demanded every preacher to be "ready to pray, ready to preach, ready to die." That is always the spirit of Christianity.

—JOHN G. LAKE

POINTS TO PONDER

In some places of the world religious persecution is not a daily reality. In other places it is. Some have to hide their faith from the authorities, meeting in secret house churches or literally underground. In these individuals rests a willingness for daily risk—a willingness to die for faith.

Matt 24 -

- How real is the threat of dying for your faith in your life?

- If you were to live in a place where the threat was real, how do you think you would respond?

- How would you describe your struggle to be willing to die for Christ?

- Read the following verses and write down in your prayer journal what they say about dying to self:

  - 2 Chronicles 7:14

  - Psalm 51:1–19

  - Matthew 10:39–42

  - Matthew 16:25–26

  - Romans 12:1–2

  - Galatians 2:20

  - Philippians 2:1–11

  - Philippians 3:7–9

Pray...

In Your hands, Lord Jesus, I put my life to be used by You, whatever the cost. Amen.

Day 21
CHRIST OUR RIGHTEOUSNESS

But because of Him you are in Christ Jesus,
whom God made unto us wisdom, righteousness, sanctification, and redemption.

[1 CORINTHIANS 1:30, MEV]

HERE IS OUR position through Jesus Christ: He has become our righteousness. We have become His very sons and daughters. Yet you sing weakness, talk weakness, pray weakness, and sing unbelief. You are like that good old woman. She said, "I do love that doctrine of falling from grace, and I practice it all the time." Another man said, "Brother, I believe in the dual nature. I believe that when I would do good, evil is always present with me, and I thank God that evil is always there."

You live it and you believe it, and God cannot do anything with you. You magnify failure, and you deify failure until, to the majority of you, the devil is bigger than God.

If you look in the Book of Genesis, you will see the size of God. It is a full-size photograph. And when you see Jesus Christ rising from the dead, you have seen the God-sized photograph of redemption. We reign as kings in the realm of life.

Jesus has taken Satan's badge of dominion and authority that Adam had given him in the Garden of Eden. Every person that accepts Jesus Christ is identified with Him.

Jesus did it for you. He died as your substitute and representative and became your righteousness. When He put His heel on Satan's neck, He did it for you. And to you who believe Satan is conquered and defeated, Satan can holler and bellow as much as he wants to, but you withstand him in the faith of Jesus Christ.

—JOHN G. LAKE

POINTS TO PONDER

- In what ways do you magnify failure in your life?

- In what ways do you give greater credit to Satan's power in your life than perhaps he deserves?

- Draw a picture in your prayer journal that depicts the size of Satan compared to the size of God.

PRAY...

Jesus, in You the enemy has been defeated for me, and You are my righteousness and authority to reign with dominion and power. Amen.

Day 22
REDEMPTION

For you know that you were not redeemed
from your vain way of life inherited from your
fathers with perishable things, like silver or
gold, but with the precious blood of Christ, as
of a lamb without blemish and without spot.

[1 PETER 1:18-19, MEV]

THE MIND OF the world is fixed on the Redeemer. The Old
Testament Scriptures, looking forward to Christ, are particularly prolific in their description of His life, His sorrows, His sufferings, His death, and His sacrifice. All these were qualities of the Redeemer.

What redemption means is best seen by following the chain of Christ's life from the Crucifixion until now. If you want to understand the Redeemer, see Him before the cross comes into view.

The great majority of the Christian world is still weeping at the foot of the cross. The consciousness of man is fixed on the Christ who died, not on the Christ who lives. They are looking back to the Redeemer who was, not the Redeemer who is.

On this side of the cross we see all the marvel of the opposite of what we see in the Christ on the other side of the cross. On the other side of the cross we see a man of sorrows, acquainted with grief, bearing our sicknesses, and carrying our sorrows.

On this side of the cross is the victory of His resurrection, the marvel of all victories—the victory over death by which He took death captive. A living man, Himself, He came forth the conqueror of death itself, having put all things under His feet. What an ascent into triumph! What a change in His consciousness! What a distinction between the Redeemer and the redeemed!

—John G. Lake

Points to Ponder

The Cross is indeed an important symbol of our faith. Its role in the meaning of our faith is magnanimous. But we may at times make it a greater symbol than it deserves, for it is not where the story ends.

- How would you describe the relationship between the Crucifixion and the Resurrection?

- How do you regard the Cross in your own life? How large is it in the story of your faith?

- How large is the Resurrection portion of the story to your faith?

Pray...

O Redeemer, I thank You for the cross and all You did to lift me from the poverty of sin to the glorious victory! Amen.

FEAST SUNDAY
Week Four of Lent

We have just spent a week meditating on the cross of Christ and its role in our faith and daily life—how we are invited to die as Christ did and yet are encouraged to move beyond the Cross and not dwell at the foot of where Christ died, for He did not stay there. Spend some time reflecting on the impact of this week's readings.

- How has your view of the Cross changed or been challenged by this week's reflections?

- When you think of the phrase "die for Christ," how does that translate in your daily life right now?

- When you consider Christ's death for you, how is that made specific? What sins did He die for in your life?

- How would you describe your relationship with the cross of Christ?

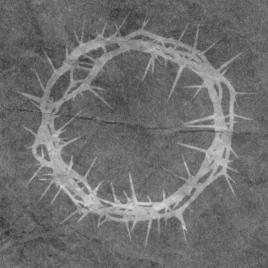

PART III

THE RESURRECTION AND ASCENSION OF CHRIST

Day 23
THE POWER OF HIS RESURRECTION

Listen, I tell you a mystery: We shall not all sleep, but we shall all be changed. In a moment, in the twinkling of an eye, at the last trumpet...

[1 CORINTHIANS 15:51–52, MEV]

NOTHING BUT THE mighty Holy Ghost will ever take you up in the clouds. He will quicken these mortal bodies, and they will be changed. We shall not have wings, but our hands and feet will be made light. Our feet shall be like "hind's feet" and we will run, skip, and almost fly. We shall know the power of the resurrection life. We shall be so filled with the Holy Ghost that our bodies will be made light. Sometimes my body is made so light, I can hardly stay.

My feet are on the earth, but my hands seem on the throne. Christ arose from the dead, and He is the resurrection and the life. People want to get the blood of Jesus over them, over their diseased bodies, in His name.

Do you believe right now? If you believe and praise the Lord in faith, it shall be done. If you do not feel the joy, offer praise as a sacrifice and ask God to give you the joy. When the unclean spirit is driven out, the disease goes and the resurrection life comes into you.

Some dance, shout, and praise the Lord as the life of Jesus thrills through them. I declare to you on the authority of God and from my own experience, I know it is the power of God through Jesus Christ. It does not take Jesus long to do the work, but it takes some of us a long time to get there. Five minutes will do the work. Then the peace of God will flow through you like a river, and you will have joy in the Holy Ghost. As you go home, do not think about your sins. Don't commit any more sins, and don't worry about the past because it is under the blood.

—MARIA WOODWORTH-ETTER

POINTS TO PONDER

Resurrection life is a free life, a lighthearted life, a joy-filled life. It is a life set free from burden and bondage. It is a life free from worry, for it knows Christ carries it all. And we can have this kind of life because of the resurrection Christ wrought from the tomb.

- Do you believe in this resurrection power and life?

- What struggles do you have to believe it?

- How do you experience the freedom of this resurrection life right now?

- Where have you experienced the peace and joy of the Holy Spirit in your life?

PRAY...

Lord Jesus Christ, I ask You for the indwelling of Your resurrection power and life. Amen.

Day 24
PRACTICING HIS PRESENCE IN PRAYER

Pray without ceasing.
[1 THESSALONIANS 5:17, MEV]

SOME MAY HAVE read the booklet by Brother Lawrence, *Practicing the Presence of Christ*. It speaks of a necessity in the Christian life—His presence that is always with us.

One of the things the Christian world does not get hold of with a strong grip is the conscious presence of Christ with us now. Somehow there is an inclination in the Christian spirit to feel that Jesus, when He left the earth and returned to glory, is not present with us now.

I want to show you how wonderfully the Scriptures emphasize the fact of His presence with us now. His promise, after the Great Commission to the eleven disciples, was, "I am with you always."

It would naturally seem as if a separation had been contemplated because of His return to glory, but no such separation is contemplated on the part of Christ. Christ promises His omnipotent presence with us always. Christ is everywhere and thus omnipresent—present in the soul, present in the world, and present unto the end of the age.

Christ is the living presence of God not only with us but to the real Christian. He is in us as the perpetual joy, power, and glory of God. When a soul reaches to the heights of God, it will only be because of the guiding, counseling, indwelling, and infilling of the Christ.

—JOHN G. LAKE

POINTS TO PONDER

To pray without ceasing is to practice God's presence constantly—anytime, anyplace, and with any kind of prayer. It's always living in a place where you are mindful of God's presence, His Spirit, within and around you. Every conversation, action, feeling, and thought is Spirit-led.

- Are you seeking God's presence in prayer all the time and in all places? Describe how this manifests itself in your life.

- When or where are some of the times or places you usually pray?

  - First thing in the morning
  - Driving the car
  - Working
  - Mowing the yard
  - Cleaning the house
  - Cooking a meal
  - Relaxing
  - Reading

  - In the shower
  - Last thing at night

- Read the following passages and describe how they encourage you to live each day in His presence:

  - Psalm 46:4–5
  - Psalm 63:1

- Psalm 90:14
- Proverbs 1:28
- Proverbs 8:17
- Lamentations 3:22–24

PRAY...

Lord Jesus, help me to remember You are with me always, closer than my own breath. Amen.

Day 25
CHRIST LIVING IN YOU

I have been crucified with Christ. It is no
longer I who live, but Christ who lives in me.
[GALATIANS 2:20, MEV]

T HAT IS THE text: "Christ liveth in me." That is the revelation of this age. That is the discovery of the moment.
That is the revolutionizing power of God in the earth. It is
the factor that is changing the spirit of religion in the world
and the character of Christian faith. It is divine vitalization.
The world is awakening to that marvelous truth, that Christ
is not in the heavens only, nor in the atmosphere only, but
Christ is in you.

—JOHN G. LAKE

POINTS TO PONDER

The world lived in darkness for thousands of years, but there
was just as much electricity in the world then as there is now.
It is not that electricity had just come into being. It was always
here, but men discovered how to utilize it and bless themselves
with it at a certain point in time.

In the same way, Christ lives in you today. You may not be
accessing the power of that reality, but it is there nonetheless.
What's more, Christ has a purpose for living in you. That purpose is to reveal Himself to you, through you, and in you.

- How would you describe the way others see Christ in you?

- How do you experience Christ living in you today?

- Spend a moment thinking on the truth that Christ lives

in you. What comes to mind as you meditate on this truth?

PRAY...

Christ, live in and through me. Amen.

Day 26
CURED OF DOUBT AND FEAR

For God has not given us the spirit of fear,
but of power, and love, and self-control.
[2 TIMOTHY 1:7, MEV]

T HE BLOOD OF Jesus is the only cure for doubt and fear. It takes sanctification to deliver a person from doubt and fear. We always find that people who are not sanctified are more or less troubled with doubt. But when they get sanctified, they are filled with such love to God that they are like little babes. They believe every word of Jesus.

Jesus had been with the disciples three-and-a-half years and had told them all about the kingdom, and yet the doubts and fears came upon them. But in Luke 24:31 we read, "And their eyes were opened, and they knew him." After the Resurrection, their spiritual eyes were opened to know Jesus.

Our eyes must be opened to see our inheritance. No one can get the baptism until Christ anoints his eyes and opens up his understanding that he might understand the Scriptures: "Then opened he their understanding, that they might understand the scriptures" (Luke 24:45). Then they received the living Word into their hearts, and their hearts burned within them as He unfolded the Scriptures to them.

Sanctification is a cure for unbelief, doubts, and fears. Jesus got all His disciples cured before He went back to glory. What do you call that but sanctification?

We can see that Jesus taught the doctrine of sanctification before He was crucified, for He had prayed that they might be sanctified in John 17. He stayed with them on earth forty days, opened their understanding, opened their eyes, and cleansed them of doubt.

—WILLIAM J. SEYMOUR

POINTS TO PONDER

We have nothing to fear, nothing to hide, and nothing to lose in following Jesus Christ. In Him are courage, truth, and abundance.

- How have doubt and fear been a part of your life thus far?
- List the things you used to doubt and fear but no longer do.
- What doubts and fears do you want to be freed from today?
- What would your life be like without those doubts and fears?

PRAY...

Jesus, empower me to conquer the spirit of fear and timidity, that I might walk in bold faith. Amen.

Understanding a gift - pray for it

Day 27
DIVINE MASTERY THROUGH CHRIST

I am He who lives, though I was dead.
Look! I am alive forevermore. Amen. And
I have the keys of Hades and of Death.
[REVELATION 1:18, MEV]

WHEN THE LORD Jesus Christ is born indeed in our souls and we yield ourselves to God by the grace and power of the Son of God, our natures possess that Spirit which is in Christ (Rom. 8:11). Then we begin to realize the spirit of mastery that Jesus possessed. That is the reason I do not spend much time talking about the devil. The Lord took care of him, bless God! Jesus has the keys of hell and of death, and He has mastered the enemy once and for all.

If you and I had as much faith to believe that the enemy is mastered as we have to believe that the Lord Jesus Christ is our Savior, we would have mighty little trouble with the devil or his power while we walk through this old world. Jesus said, "Behold, I give unto you power to tread on serpents and scorpions, and over all the power of the enemy: and nothing shall by any means hurt you" (Luke 10:19).

It is not worthwhile talking about an enemy after he is wiped out. It is a hard thing for the Christian mind to conceive that the power of evil is really a vanquished power.

Beloved, you and I have bowed our heads before a vanquished enemy. We have failed through lack of faith to comprehend that Christ is the Master. He who dares by the grace of God to look into the face of the Lord Jesus Christ knows within his own soul the divine mastery that the Christ of God is exercising now.

—John G. Lake

Points to Ponder

We spend a lot of time thinking of the ways Christ has changed us forever. It happened through the Cross. It happened through the Resurrection. It happened through the Ascension. It happened through the demonstration of His own life, how He shows us kingdom life. But what about the devil? Christ's victory is just as much about him because of the power He stripped from our enemy's hands.

- What does it mean for our enemy to have been mastered by Christ?

- How is the enemy's loss real in your life?

- How are you living as though the enemy still holds power?

Pray...

Lord, help me to see myself as You see me: more than a conqueror in You. Amen.

Day 28
SHUT OUT EVIL

Look, I give you authority to trample on serpents
and scorpions, and over all the power of the
enemy. And nothing shall by any means hurt you.
[LUKE 10:19, MEV]

I TELL YOU, BELOVED, it is not necessary for people to be dominated by evil, nor by evil spirits. Instead of being dominated, Christians should exercise dominion and control other forces. Even Satan has no power over them, only as they permit him to have. Jesus taught us to close the mind, to close the heart, to close the being against all that is evil and to live with an openness to God only, so that the sunlight and glory-radiance of God shines in and shuts out everything that is dark.

Jesus said, "Take heed therefore how ye hear" (Luke 8:18)—not what you hear. One cannot help *what* he hears, but he can take heed *how* he hears. When it is something offensive to the Spirit and to the knowledge of God, shut the doors against it and it will not touch you.

The Christian lives as God wills in the world, dominating sin, evil, and sickness. I would to God that He would be lifted up until all believers would realize their privilege in Christ Jesus.

By the Spirit within us, we cast out or expel from our beings all that is not God-like. If you find within your heart a thought of sin or selfishness, by the exercise of the Spirit of God within you, cast that thing out as unworthy of a child of God and put it away from you. God says to us, "Be ye holy; for I am holy" (1 Pet. 1:16).

—JOHN G. LAKE

POINTS TO PONDER

- How would you describe your level of dominion over dark forces of temptation in your life?

- Which of the things below do you need to shut the door to in your life?
  - Anger
  - Bitterness
  - Dishonoring parents
  - Fear
  - Gossip
  - Greed
  - Idolatry
  - Immorality
  - Laziness
  - Lust
  - Materialism
  - Pornography
  - Pride
  - Substance abuse
  - The occult
  - Unbelief
  - Workaholism
  - Other:

- Which might be a source of attack and unholiness in your life? Are you willing to do away with it? Rank those things below that bring profanity into your life. (Rank from one to ten, with ten being very tempting and profane.)

- Magazines
- Movies and videos
- Music
- News
- Talk radio
- Television
- Other:

• On a scale of one to ten, how willing are you to shut the door to every evil that tempts and attacks you? Why is that your level of willingness?

PRAY...

Jesus, by Your Spirit, I cast out all unholiness, sin, and selfishness from my life as unworthy for a child of God. I shut the door of my ears to anything unholy. Amen.

FEAST SUNDAY
Week Five of Lent

Our focus this week has been the resurrection power of Christ. Because of Christ's resurrection, we have access not only to Christ Himself, alive and well, but also to a greater power to overcome the wiles of our enemy. Take some time to reflect on what you've learned this week.

- How important has the Resurrection been in your faith prior to this week's study?

- How would you describe its importance now?

- What needs to change in terms of accessing the power of Christ's resurrection in your life?

- Write a prayer in your journal that expresses your desire for greater resurrection power in your life.

Day 29
GOD'S RESURRECTION TOUCH

Then Peter said, "I have no silver and gold,
but I give you what I have. In the name of
Jesus Christ of Nazareth, rise up and walk."

[ACTS 3:6, MEV]

A MAN WHO HAD spent years in a wheelchair but who had been healed came on the platform and told how he was loosed. Another person with a blood issue for many years testified. A blind man told how he got his eyes opened.

I said to the people, "Are you ready?" Oh, they were so ready. A dear man got hold of a boy who was encased in iron from top to bottom, lifted him up, and placed him on the platform. Hands were laid upon him in the name of Jesus.

"Papa! Papa! Papa!" he said. "It's all over me! O Papa, come take these irons off!" And the father took the irons off. Healing had gone all over the boy.

This is what I feel. The life of God is going all over me, the power of God is all over me.

Let it go over us, Lord, the power of the Holy Ghost, the resurrection of heaven, the sweetness of His benediction, and the joy of the Lord!

—SMITH WIGGLESWORTH

POINTS TO PONDER

When we think about the resurrection of Christ, we often think of it as a single event in history—a moment in time when Christ rose from the dead. It's less common for us to think of it as something continually happening and even applying to our lives. But that's what this reading teaches us: God's touch *is* resurrection. It brings resurrection to our own lives. In this, we participate in the greatest event in history.

- When you think of resurrection, what comes to mind?

- How do you think God wants the resurrection to be part of your life today?

- What would God's resurrection touch in your life look like?

- Where have you seen God's resurrection touch at work around you?

PRAY...

Touch me, Lord, with Thy resurrection power, Thy blessing, and Thy joy. Amen.

Day 30
THE VISION OF THE DIVINE REALITY

Then the eyes of the blind shall be opened,
and the ears of the deaf shall be unstopped.
Then the lame man shall leap as a deer, and
the tongue of the mute sing for joy.

[Isaiah 35:5–6, mev]

I CAN UNDERSTAND THE thrill that must have moved David when he sang the 103rd Psalm: "Bless the LORD, O my soul, and forget not all his benefits: who forgiveth all thine iniquities; who healeth all thy diseases" (Ps. 103:2–3).

The vision that has called forth the shouts of praise from the souls of men in all ages is the same vision that stirs your heart and mine today. It is the vision of the divine reality of the salvation of Jesus Christ by which the greatness of God's purpose in Him is revealed to mankind, by the Spirit of the living One. By that great salvation, we are transformed, lifted, and unified with the living Christ through the Holy Ghost so that all the parts, energies, and functions of the nature of Jesus Christ are revealed through man unto the salvation of the world.

The vision of God's relation to man and man's relation to God is changing the character of Christianity from a groveling something, weeping and wailing its way in tears, to the kingly recognition of union and communion with the living One of God.

I am glad, bless God, that the Scriptures have dignified us with that marvelous title of "sons of God" (John 1:12). I am glad there is such a relation as a "son of God" and that by His grace the soul is cleansed by the precious blood of Jesus Christ, filled, and energized by His own kingly Spirit. By the grace of God, a saved person has become God's king, God's gentleman in deed and in truth.

—JOHN G. LAKE

POINTS TO PONDER

Through the Resurrection we are invited to esteem our faith high and grand, not "groveling … weeping and wailing its way in tears."

- How is your faith high and grand, full of celebration?
- How do groveling, weeping, and wailing make their way into your faith expression too?
- Why do you think they show up?
- Write a prayer that expresses to God your desire to be free from anything that hinders you from a grand and high celebration of your faith.

PRAY…

I praise You, Lord Jesus, for imparting Your royalty to my nature. In You, I am royalty—a child of the King. Amen.

Day 31
A LIFE OF HOLY TRIUMPH

No, in all these things we are more than conquerors through Him who loved us.

[ROMANS 8:37, MEV]

O NE OF THE truest things in all my life in my relationship
with the Lord Jesus Christ has been to feel that He was
capable of knowing my sorrows and yours. And in the truest
sense, He thereby became our comrade.

In the Book of Isaiah, there is a verse that wonderfully
expresses that fact: "In all their affliction he was afflicted, and
the angel of his presence saved them: in his love and in his pity
he redeemed them; and he bare them, and carried them all the
days of old" (Isa. 63:9).

There is a union between the Christ and the Christian that
is so deep, so pure, so sweet, so real that the very conditions of
the human spirit are transmitted to His and the conditions of
the Christ's Spirit are transmitted to ours. It is because of the
continuous inflow of the Spirit of Christ in our hearts that we
appreciate or realize His power and triumph. His Spirit lifts
us above [our] surroundings and causes us to triumph anywhere and everywhere.

The Christian life is designed by God to be a life of splendid,
holy triumph. That triumph is produced in us through the continuous inflow and abiding presence of the Spirit of the trium-
phant Christ. He brings into our nature the triumph that He
enjoys. Indeed, the mature Christian, having entered into that
consciousness of overcoming through the Spirit of Christ, is

privileged to transmit that same overcoming power and spirit to other lives, in and through the power of the Spirit of God.

—John G. Lake

Points to Ponder

Christ as comrade. The Christian life as splendid, holy triumph. Could anything be better than these? You are invited to know Christ as closer than a brother. Through that intimacy you also gain a greater scope of authority to overcome in this life.

- How do you experience Christ as comrade?

- In what ways are you experiencing a life of splendid, holy triumph?

- In what areas do you need a greater reality of that triumph?

Pray...

In my life, Lord Jesus, bring triumph and victory over the enemy, that I might glorify You for every holy triumph. Amen.

Day 32
ONLY IN CHRIST IS THERE LIFE

In Him was life, and the life was
the light of mankind.
[JOHN 1:4, MEV]

Do you know we do not read the Scriptures like people read a textbook? Have you ever observed how a scientist reads his textbook? He weighs every single word, and each word has a peculiar meaning.

If we read the Word of God like that, we would get the real vitality of what it says. I wonder if we have caught the force of this Scripture: "Paul, an apostle of Jesus Christ by the will of God, according to the promise of life which is in Christ Jesus" (2 Tim. 1:1).

There is no life outside of Jesus Christ, no eternal life outside of Jesus Christ, by the declaration of Jesus Himself. John said: "God hath given to us eternal life, and this life is in his Son. He that hath the Son hath life: and he that hath not the Son of God hath not life" (1 John 5:11–12).

Observe these words: "According to the promise of life." There is no promise of life outside of Jesus Christ. Jesus was the most emphatic teacher the world ever saw. He said: "Ye must be born again" (John 3:7). There is no arbitration by which you can get around the matter. There is no possibility of avoiding that truth. You have got to come straight to it and meet it. "According to the promise of life which is in Christ Jesus."

—JOHN G. LAKE

Points to Ponder

You are promised life through Christ Jesus. *Life.* And not just life in the here and now but also life in eternity. For you death and oblivion are not the ultimate reality. They have no staying power. For you it is all about life.

- When you think of the word *life,* what comes to mind?

- What is the significance of being a person of life rather than death?

- How is your life in the here and now affected by this promise of God?

Pray...

Jesus, I confess that in You alone is life. Amen.

Day 33
JESUS'S BRIDE

That He might present it to Himself a glorious church, not having spot, or wrinkle,
or any such thing, but that it should
be holy and without blemish.

[EPHESIANS 5:27, MEV]

Gᴏᴅ ɪꜱ ᴘʀᴇᴘᴀʀɪɴɢ His spiritual ark today. The body of
Christ will soon be complete, and when it is complete it
will go above the treetops to meet our Lord and King in the
air. We are in the day of preparation of the King of glory, and
His bride is making herself ready. Rejoice and be glad, for the
marriage of the Lamb is at hand. The bride must be arrayed in
white linen and the robe of righteousness, clothed in the power
of the Holy Spirit.

She is getting her garments ready to meet the Bridegroom.
I praise the Lord that I am living in this day. The bride will
be caught up just before the tribulation bursts upon this sin-
cursed earth. The bride must be very beautiful. She is repre-
sented as a queen dressed in a robe of finest needlework. She
will shine with the gifts and jewels of the Holy Ghost.

We have this treasure in earthen vessels. But they that be
wise shall shine as the brightness of the sun, and the wise shall
know when these things are coming, when the ark is about ready
to go up. The Lord will not keep any secrets from them, as there
is perfect confidence between the bride and the Bridegroom. So
Jesus will reveal secrets to His bride.

A bride is very happy. She is willing to forsake her father's
house, her friends, everything, and go with her Bridegroom,

even to a foreign country. She loves those she leaves, but He is dearer to her than anything else.

The bride will be taken out, and men and women will be left. You may say, "I do not believe it." I believe it!

—MARIA WOODWORTH-ETTER

POINTS TO PONDER

It is no small thing to be called the bride of Christ. A bride is wanted. A bride is invited into a new life. A bride makes preparations for the special day ahead. A bride is considered the most beautiful and fair of all on that day. In her time of preparation she is cherished and celebrated. On her day of celebration she is held in highest regard. And following the wedding feast she enters into a lifetime of intimacy and shared life with her beloved.

- How do you experience yourself as the bride of Christ now in preparation for the wedding day ahead?

- How do you experience yourself as wanted and invited into a new life ahead with your Bridegroom?

- What do you love about your Bridegroom?

PRAY...

Lord Jesus, prepare Your bride, the church, for the wedding feast. Amen.

Day 34
JESUS IS COMING QUICKLY

He who testifies to these things
says, "Surely I am coming soon."
[REVELATION 22:20, MEV]

CHRIST WILL COME as quickly as the lightning flashes from the east to the west, and just as quickly He will snatch His bridal company away while the world sleeps in a drunken stupor.

But the next time He comes, all will know it. Every knee shall bow, and every tongue shall confess Jesus Christ as Lord (Phil. 2:10–11). Every eye shall see Him, and every slanderous tongue will have to confess before the world that these were God's chosen vessels.

This honor belongs to the saints. The world will have to confess that we were right and that they were wrong. God is very proud of His bride. God's children now deny themselves many of the things of the world, but they are heirs of the kingdom, even though many are poor in this world and having hard times. There is going to be a change in this old world. God is calling you to behold. Don't go a step further.

The first time, the bride will be caught away. The second time, she will come riding on white horses. Jesus will stand on the Mount of Olives, and they that pierced Him shall see Him. You now know down in your hearts that Jesus is the Christ. God's people hear something more than natural men hear. The wisdom we get comes from God, who gives liberally to all His people. More than anything else my prayer has been, "Give me wisdom." A blind man can see if he looks with spiritual eyes at the signs of the times.

—MARIA WOODWORTH-ETTER

POINTS TO PONDER

Though we live in a time of turbulence and doubt, there will come a day when none shall doubt again. All will know the Christ. All will fall at His feet. And those of us who are His bride will be caught into eternal glory and unending joy.

- What is it like for you to live in the waiting period until that day?

- Who are those you want to know and acknowledge the real and living Christ on that day?

- Is there anything you want to ask from God as you wait until the final revelation? Write a prayer, asking God for it now.

PRAY...

Lord, I am ready and waiting for the day when You will come and take Your bride. Amen.

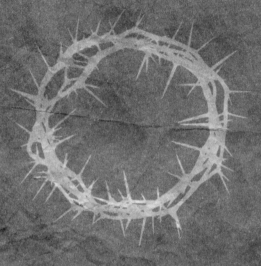

PART IV

HOLY WEEK

PALM SUNDAY

They brought the colt to Jesus and threw their
garments on it. And He sat upon it. Many spread
their garments on the street. And others cut down
branches off the trees and scattered them on the
street. Those who went before and those who followed cried out, saying: "Hosanna! 'Blessed is He
who comes in the name of the Lord!' Blessed is
the kingdom of our father David that is coming
in the name of the Lord! Hosanna in the highest!"

[MARK 11:7–10, MEV]

TODAY WE BEGIN our meditation on the final week in the
life of Jesus—what the church has historically termed
Holy Week.

It begins with Palm Sunday. On this day in the life of
Christ He entered into the city of Jerusalem on the back of a
donkey with all the palms and hosannas of the people show-
ered before and behind him. He was celebrated and hailed on
this day, even as His death loomed ahead of Him, less than a
week away. Those who praised His name on this Palm Sunday
would leave Him alone and ridiculed and sentenced to die in
just a few short days.

- Activate your imagination and allow your mind's eye to
  see the scene quoted here from Mark 11. How is your
  sense of smell activated by this scene? What about your
  sense of touch? How about your sense of hearing?

- Can you imagine yourself in this scene anywhere? If you'd been there that day, where would you have found yourself? What would you have been doing and saying?

- What do you imagine the people in this scene are longing for?

- How do you see Jesus responding to the crowd?

Day 35
NOT I, BUT CHRIST

Then Peter said, "I have no silver and gold,
but I give you what I have. In the name of
Jesus Christ of Nazareth, rise up and walk."
[ACTS 3:6, MEV]

IN THE NEW Testament, signs and wonders were done before the people. Wherever Jesus went, the people followed Him. God was with Him, putting fear upon the people through miracles, signs, and wonders that God wrought through Him.

He said, "I speak not of myself: but the Father that dwelleth in me, he doeth the works" (John 14:10). When the rulers, elders, and scribes demanded to know from Peter, "By what power, or by what name, have ye done this?" Peter responded, "Be it known unto you all, and to all the people of Israel, that by the name of Jesus Christ of Nazareth, whom ye crucified, whom God raised from the dead, even by him doth this man stand here before you whole" (Acts 4:7, 10). Not I, but Christ. It is the same today.

In the signs and wonders today, it is "Not I, but Christ." He dwells in these bodies, and the work is done by the mighty power of the Holy Ghost. "Know ye not that your body is the temple of the Holy Ghost?" Jesus Christ dwells in us. We are God's powerhouse.

—MARIA WOODWORTH-ETTER

POINTS TO PONDER

How does Christ perform miracles today? Through us. We are His tabernacles and His dwelling places. However, we do not heal; Christ heals. We do not work miracles; Christ is the miracle worker. Never touch His glory. In Him all things are possible. Apart from Christ nothing is possible.

- What would have made you follow Christ around, just as the people in His day did, if you had been there at the time?

- What miracles have you witnessed in your lifetime?

- Make a list in your prayer journal of all the miracles— large or small—that have happened in your life over the last week.

PRAY...

Jesus, I desire to be Your powerhouse. Amen.

Day 36
GROWING IN CHRIST

For this reason we do not lose heart: Even
though our outward man is perishing, yet our
inward man is being renewed day by day.
[2 CORINTHIANS 4:16, MEV]

SALVATION TO MY heart is Christ's glorious reality. Under a
tree away back in Canada one night I knelt and poured out
my heart to God and asked Him by His grace to take possession of my life and nature and make me a Christian man and
let me know the power of His salvation. And Christ was born
in my soul. Such a joy of God possessed my heart that the
leaves of the trees seemed to dance for months following, and
the birds sang a new song.

Salvation is a progressive condition. The difficulty with the
church has been that men were induced to confess their sins to
Christ and acknowledge Him as a Savior, and there they stopped,
there they petrified, there they withered, there they died—dry-
rotted. I believe in these phases I have expressed the real thing
that has taken place in 85 percent of professing Christians in
the world. Oh, bless God, we never saw Christ's intention.

Yea, bless God, there came a day when God once more in His
loving mercy endowed me with the Spirit of God to be and perform the things that He had planted in my soul and had revealed
in His own blessed Word and life.

I invite you to this life of divine reality. I invite you to enter
into the Lord Jesus. I invite you to enter into His nature, that

you may know Him, for no man can say that Jesus is the Lord but by the Holy Ghost.

—JOHN G. LAKE

POINTS TO PONDER

The salvation Christ intends is much greater than we have imagined. It is a gift of life, and it is meant to fill us up and change our nature more and more as we go. It was never intended to be a onetime event. It was and is intended to change your life continually.

- How would you describe your understanding of salvation?

- How is that similar or different from what has been described here?

- In your journal list some of your own "leaf-dancing" moments of faith—moments when your life in God became truly real and deep.

PRAY...

Change me daily, Lord, that I might grow and be renewed. Amen.

Day 37

BEING IN PRAYER

Therefore, if any man is in Christ, he is a
new creature. Old things have passed
away. Look, all things have become new.

[2 CORINTHIANS 5:17, MEV]

BUT THE SECRET of Christianity is not in doing. The secret is in being. Real Christianity is in being a possessor of the nature of Jesus Christ. In other words, it is being Christ in character, Christ in demonstration, and Christ in agency of transmission. When one gives himself to the Lord and becomes a child of God, all that he does and all that he says from that time on should be the will, the words, and the actions of Jesus, just as absolutely and as entirely as Jesus spoke and did the will of the Father.

Jesus showed us that the only way to live this life was to commit oneself, as He did, to the will of God. He did not walk in His own ways at all but walked in God's ways. So the one who is going to be a Christian in the best sense and let the world see Jesus in him must walk in all the ways of Jesus by following Him. He must be a Christ-man or Christ-woman—a Christian, or Christ-one.

—JOHN G. LAKE

POINTS TO PONDER

What are you trying to do for God? If it's you trying, then stop trying and start trusting. If what you are doing for God is in your own strength, then nothing will happen. If what you are

97

doing for God is rooted in His strength, will, and love, then your prayers will move mountains.

Surrendering to God's will is not a process of doing but of being, not a matter of trying but of trusting, and not an act of achieving but of receiving.

- As you consider your growth into maturity as a Christian, where do you find yourself on the continuum between "trusting" and "still trying"? Are you closer to trusting or would you say you are still trying to trust?

- Are you "being" or "doing"? Or are you somewhere in between?

- What about grace? Are you receiving the grace of God or are you working to achieve His grace?

- How would you describe the "doing" aspect of your life right now?

- How would you describe the "being" aspect?

PRAY...

Jesus, help me learn to be with You and the Father in a spirit of peace and rest. Amen.

Day 38

EVEN UNTO DEATH

Take and eat. This is My body
which is broken for you.
[1 CORINTHIANS 11:24, MEV]

W E COME TO the last night of the Lord's life. He is with His disciples in the Upper Room. Here comes the final act, the consummation of all His life. There is a phase of this act I know the Lord has not made clear to many.

They sat around the table after they had eaten their supper. Jesus took bread and brake it and instructed them to take and eat. What did He mean? Since He was there in the flesh, what was the significance of the breaking of bread?

By that act, the Lord Jesus Christ pledged Himself before God, before the holy angels, and before men that He would not stop short of dying for the world. There was no limit. He was faithful even unto death.

Just as He had been faithful in life and had lived each day conscious of everything in life around Him, so now He would fix His entire being on the cross. He was going to be faithful even unto death.

The real purpose of becoming a Christian is not to save yourself from hell or to be saved to go to heaven. It is to become a child of God with the character of Jesus Christ to stand before men, pledged unto the uttermost, even unto death, by refusing to sin, refusing to bow your head in shame, preferring to die rather than to dishonor the Son of God.

If the character of Jesus Christ has entered into you and

into me, then it has made us like Him in purpose. It has made us like Him in fact. Bless God! His Spirit is imparted to us. Bless God for that same unquenchable fidelity that character- ized the Son of God.

—JOHN G. LAKE

POINTS TO PONDER

One of the most awe-inspiring aspects of Christ's personality is His single-minded focus to complete what He intends to do. We see this in His ministry of preaching and healing, and we see it here at the end of His life. What's more, He intends to grow this same quality of faithful focus in you.

- What would you say the breaking of the bread signifies?

- How do you see single-minded focus and faithfulness at play in your own life?

- How might such focus and faithfulness need to grow when it comes to your faith?

PRAY...

Jesus, for me to live or die for You is gain. Amen.

Day 39

VICTORY FOLLOWS CRUCIFIXION

No, in all these things we are more than conquerors through Him who loved us.

[Romans 8:37, mev]

Think of what hung on that momentous hour that Jesus suffered. No hour in all history has been fraught with such eternal interests. It was a crucial hour, and He was a willing offering. He said, "What shall I say? Father, save me from this hour: but for this cause came I unto this hour" (John 12:27).

There is a crucial hour in every man and woman's life. Someone now may be facing their cross, their Gethsemane. Will you say, "Father, save me from this hour"?

You know the blessing that came when Jesus endured the cross, despising the shame. Face the hour of opportunity. Some are drawing back. God will give you grace for the hour of your opportunity. Let us pray, "Lord, save me from drawing back."

Our Christ, who went every step of the way, says, "I will never leave you or forsake you." When we get on the resurrection side of the cross, the glory and victory will be unspeakable.

—William J. Seymour

Points to Ponder

Can you allow yourself to enter into that fateful hour with Christ? Imagine being fully aware that your death looms near. Imagine knowing the loneliness and pain that lies ahead. Imagine the moment of decision: Will you step forward?

In that fateful hour Christ wanted His fate to change. He wanted the Father to find some other way. It was a struggle for the relinquishment of His will. Eventually He surrendered— and the entire fate of humanity and history changed.

- As you allowed yourself to imagine that fateful hour with Christ, what did you see, think, and feel?

- Have you ever faced a crucial point of decision? What was it about? What happened?

- Where do you struggle to be faithful to the end with Christ?

PRAY...

Lord Jesus, save me from drawing back. Give me the strength to die to self, that I might live for You. Amen.

Day 40

PRAYING THE CROSS

God forbid that I should boast, except in the
cross of our Lord Jesus Christ, by whom the
world is crucified to me, and I to the world.

[GALATIANS 6:14, MEV]

M EN HAVE SAID that the cross of Christ was not a heroic
thing, but I want to tell you that the cross of Jesus Christ
has put more heroism in the souls of men than any other event
in human history. Men have lived, rejoiced, and died believing
in the living God, in the Christ of God whose blood cleansed
their hearts from sin, and who have realized the real high spirit
of His holy sacrifice, bless God.

They manifested to mankind that same measure of sacrifice
and endured all that human beings could endure. When endur-
ance was no longer possible, they passed on to be with God,
leaving the world blessed through the evidence of a consecration
deep and true and pure and good, like the Son of God Himself.

—JOHN G. LAKE

POINTS TO PONDER

- Praying the Cross begins with repentance—turning
  away from sin and the world and to Jesus Christ. Read
  the following passages and describe what they say about
  repentance:

  - Matthew 4:17
  - Acts 2:38

- Acts 3:19
- 2 Corinthians 7:10

- Praying the Cross inspires confession—agreeing with God that we are sinners and need the Savior, Jesus Christ. Describe what each of the following verses says about confession:

  - Matthew 10:32
  - Romans 10:9
  - Philippians 2:11
  - 1 John 1:9

- Praying the Cross demands sacrifice—offering ourselves totally in surrender to Christ. Read the following verses and write down in your journal what the Bible says about sacrifice:

  - Psalm 51:16–17
  - Romans 12:1–2
  - Galatians 2:20

PRAY...

Jesus, I lay at the foot of Your cross all my sin and weakness. Cleanse me with Your blood, and empower me to take up my cross and follow You, whatever the cost. Amen.

Zech
14:12-16

RESURRECTION DAY

Jesus said to her, "Woman, why are you weeping?
Whom are you seeking?" Supposing Him to
be the gardener, she said to Him, "Sir, if You
have carried Him away, tell me where You have
put Him, and I will take Him away." Jesus said
to her, "Mary." She turned and said to Him,
"Rabboni!" (which means Teacher). Jesus said to
her, "Stop holding on to Me, for I have not yet
ascended to My Father. But go to My brothers
and tell them, 'I am ascending to My Father
and your Father, to My God and your God.'"

[JOHN 20:15–17, MEV]

RESURRECTION DAY! WHAT a day of joy this is! We cele-
brate the waking of our Lord from death to new life, from
crucifixion to victory.

What a marvel that Christ should choose to make Himself
known to Mary Magdalene first of all, and that without her
first knowing who He was. He met her in her weeping and
turned her tears to joy. Then He sent her off to tell the news
to the others.

- What do you imagine it was like for Mary Magdalene
  to meet upon the resurrected Christ and to know Him
  as her beloved teacher—and yet different than He
  was before? How do you suppose He might have been
  different?

- If you were to meet upon Christ in the garden this way,
  what do you imagine you would say to Him?

- If He asked you to leave His presence and tell the others, would that have been easy or difficult for you to do? Why is that?

- How is the reality of the Resurrection impacting your faith on this day?